For our first child, whose arrival in June of 1992 we are eagerly awaiting.

Special thanks to my talented Editorial Review Staff: Beth and Rick, Mom and Dad, Keith, Laura, Jim and Debbie, Nan and Carlos, Lucy and Dave, Bob and Kay, Don and Kathy, Chuck and Jeannie, the Man from Schaad, and the Saranac Lake Gang: Don and Mary, Bobby and Debbie, Greg and Liz, Ann and Pete, Amy and Dave, and Devin and Allison

Thanks to back cover models: Michael Kane, Jamie Kane, McKenzie Robb, Hayley Robb, Jennifer Dowd, Katie Woolley, Emily deRedon, Kelsey Robb, Taylor Kane, Samuel Kane, and Alexandra Feldman. Back cover photography by Steve Robb

Front cover watercolor by Laura McPherson

McPHERSON ON PARENTING

JOHN McPHERSON

ZondervanPublishingHouse

Grand Rapids, Michigan

A Division of HarperCollinsPublishers

McPherson on Parenting
Copyright © 1992 by John McPherson

Requests for information should be addressed to:
Zondervan Publishing House
Grand Rapids, Michigan 49530

Library of Congress Cataloging-in-Publication Data

McPherson, John, 1959–
    McPherson on parenting / John McPherson
        p.   cm.
    ISBN 0-310-58071-4 (pbk.)
    1. Parenting—Caricatures and cartoons. 2. American wit and humor.
    Pictorial. I. Title
    NC1429.M275A4 1992
    741.5'973—dc20   91-40312
                                                                              CIP

Many of the cartoons in this book originally appeared in *The Saturday Evening Post,*
Yankee, The Chronicle of Glens Falls, Marriage Partnership, Today's Christian Woman,
and *Physician's Management.* Many thanks to these publications for the support they
have given me over the last several years and for their permission in allowing us to
reprint some of these cartoons.

Printed in the United States of America

92   93   94   95   96   97   98 / CH / 10   9   8   7   6   5   4   3   2   1

"YEAH, I KNOW YOUR CONTRACTIONS ARE ONLY TWO MINUTES APART. BUT IF YOU CAN JUST HANG IN THERE UNTIL TOMORROW, I'LL WIN THE BABY POOL AT WORK."

"WELL, I'D LIKE TO _SEE_ THE SECTION IN YOUR HEALTH BOOK THAT SAYS PREGNANT WOMEN SHOULDN'T COOK."

"HERE YOU CAN CLEARLY SEE THE BABY'S HEAD AND ... OH LOOK! HE'S WIGGLING HIS TOES THERE!"

UNABLE TO DECIDE ON A NAME FOR THEIR BABY, STEVE AND KIM ROBB LEAVE IT TO FATE.

"I WANT TO START GETTING USED TO THIS BACKPACK BEFORE THE BABY COMES ALONG."

"SORRY ABOUT THE MIX-UP, MR. PENDLETON. WE'LL BE MOVING YOU TO ANOTHER ROOM SHORTLY."

MCPHERSON

"THIS IS FRANK'S *FIRST TIME* CHANGING THE BABY'S DIAPER."

"HEY, YOU WANT HER TO SLEEP THROUGH THE NIGHT, DON'T YOU?"

"THIS IS _NOT_ WHAT I HAD IN MIND WHEN I ASKED YOU TO TAKE THE BABY FOR A STROLL!"

"THAT'S THE BABY'S THERMOMETER."

"YOU'VE HAD A LOT ON YOUR MIND LATELY, HAVEN'T YOU HOWARD?"

"AND THIS LITTLE PIGGY FAKED LEFT AND RAN UP THE MIDDLE FOR A TWENTY-EIGHT YARD GAIN."

"I KNOW THIS IS A BIT UNUSUAL, MRS. GLENMONT. BUT SINCE WE'VE NEVER HIRED A BABYSITTER BEFORE I'M SURE YOU CAN UNDERSTAND THAT WE'RE JUST TAKING SOME PRECAUTIONS.

"FIVE MONTHS AND YOU STILL HAVEN'T FIGURED OUT HOW TO UNFOLD THE STROLLER!"

"I READ SOMEWHERE THAT A TYPICAL BABY REQUIRES 10,000 DIAPER CHANGES BEFORE IT'S POTTY TRAINED. SO FAR I'M UP TO 302."

"NO, I DON'T MEAN SHE'S GOT MY NOSE! I MEAN, SHE'S GOT MY NOSE!!"

THE POCKET SLIDE PROJECTOR: AN EXCITING NEW DEVELOPMENT FOR FIRST-TIME PARENTS, A CURSE FOR THEIR ACQUAINTANCES.

"WHAT ARE YOU GLARING AT ME FOR?! HE LOVES THIS, AND THIS TERRY-CLOTH OUTFIT HE'S WEARING IS PERFECT FOR WAXING THE CAR."

"WE NEED TO CUT DOWN ON THOSE CALCIUM SUPPLEMENTS."

THE DREAM APPLIANCE FOR NEW PARENTS.

"WARREN FOUND THAT HE CAN GET THE BABY TO STOP CRYING IF HE HOLDS HER AT A 45 DEGREE ANGLE WHILE HOPPING CLOCK-WISE ON ONE FOOT AND SINGS 'SOME ENCHANTED EVENING'."

"WILL YOU _DO_ SOMETHING ABOUT HIM?!!"

"I'M GOING OVER TO THE HALMS' TO BORROW A CUP OF SUGAR. IN CASE THERE'S A PROBLEM, THEIR PHONE NUMBER IS ON THE REFRIGERATOR. THE DOCTOR'S NUMBER IS IN THE BOOK. IF THOSE LINES ARE BUSY, CALL MY MOTHER. I'LL BE BACK IN TWO MINUTES."

"TWO OR THREE MONTHS AGO I WAS ALWAYS EXHAUSTED BECAUSE HE NEEDED CONSTANT ATTENTION. NOW THAT HE'S ABLE TO ENTERTAIN HIMSELF, LIFE IS _SO_ MUCH EASIER."

"DAN FOUND A WAY TO WIRE THE BABY MONITOR INTO THE STEREO."

"AND HERE'S A PIECE OF EQUIPMENT YOU'RE GOING TO GET TO KNOW REAL WELL, DANNY. THAT'S IT, GET USED TO THE FEEL OF THE HANDLE."

HOW TO TODDLER-PROOF YOUR HOME.

"WONDERFUL. WE SPEND EIGHT HUNDRED DOLLARS ON TOYS AND SHE PLAYS WITH A SHOE BOX FOR THREE DAYS NON-STOP."

"AND OVER HERE WE HAVE TYLER'S 'BLUE PERIOD'. NOTICE THE STRONG, SWEEPING STROKES THAT SEEM TO LEAP RIGHT OFF THE CANVAS."

"LEAVE THE KITTY ALONE, DEAR."

"WAIT A SECOND! THAT'S NOT THE TOY LAWN MOWER!"

"I GOT SICK AND TIRED OF PUTTING HER IN AND OUT OF THE CAR SEAT SO I FINALLY JUST SAID 'THE HECK WITH IT'."

"ALL RIGHT NOW, GIVE MOMMY THE SUPER GLUE."

"NO, THEY DIDN'T WIN THE LOTTERY. THEIR THREE-YEAR OLD JUST GOT POTTY-TRAINED."

TOY-VAC 2000

"I'M CONCERNED ABOUT HIS THUMB-SUCKING."

"UHH..EXCUSE ME MA'AM, BUT YOU'VE...UH..TAKEN MY CART BY MISTAKE. I BELIEVE THAT'S YOURS OVER THERE."

"WILL YOU JUST PICK ONE! HE'S NEVER GOING TO RECOGNIZE IT!"

"ELLEN, GO OVER AND HELP YOUR FATHER GET THE CHILD-PROOF CAP OFF THE ASPIRIN."

"REMEMBER THE GOOD OLD DAYS WHEN YOU COULD JUST TIE AN OLD TIRE TO A TREE BRANCH?"

"HE DOES NOT HAVE A DISCIPLINE PROBLEM. HE'S JUST HAD A LITTLE TOO MUCH SUGAR, THAT'S ALL."

TRICK-OR-TREATING GOES HI-TECH.

"WE WERE RUNNING OUT OF ROOM FOR THE KIDS' DRAWINGS, SO WE HAD TO GET ANOTHER REFRIGERATOR."

"I DON'T THINK YOU NEED TO PUSH QUITE SO HARD, DAD."

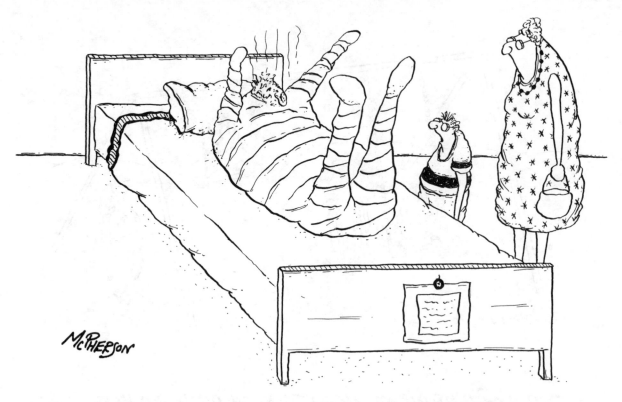

"ARE YOU GONNA MAKE ME RETURN THE CHEMISTRY SET?"

"I'VE TOLD YOU TIME AND TIME AGAIN NEVER TO LEAVE TOYS ON THE STAIRS! I COULD HAVE TRIPPED ON THAT AND BROKEN MY ARM!"

"WHATEVER YOU DO, DON'T TELL MOM HE'S IN HERE."

"YOU GUYS DIDN'T HAPPEN TO SEE MY SCIENCE PROJECT COME CRAWLING THROUGH HERE, DID YOU?"

"...SOMEWHERE ALONG THE LINE WE'VE FAILED AS PARENTS."

"THEY'RE DONE! HAHA! ALL THE SCHOOL LUNCHES ARE DONE FOR THE NEXT 186 DAYS! NO MORE GETTING UP AT 6 A.M! NO MORE MESSY SANDWICHES! NO MORE..."

"I'VE GOT THE THING WIRED UP TO A GENERATOR IN THE BASEMENT. WE CUT OUR ELECTRIC BILL IN HALF LAST YEAR."

"THERE, NOW. DO YOU SEE WHAT HAPPENS WHEN WE DON'T LEARN TO SHARE?"

"WELL, THANK YOU, WAYNE AND ELWIN! AN _ASSAULT OF THE PSYCHO GRORKS_ NINTENDO CARTRIDGE! HOW THOUGHTFUL OF YOU."

"I TOLD YOU IT WAS A STUPID IDEA TO MAKE IT OUT OF CINDERBLOCKS!"

"I MADE THESE OUT OF LEFTOVERS FROM THANKSGIVING DINNER. THEY'RE GRAVY POPSICLES."

"SORRY, DAD. WE GOT A LITTLE CARRIED AWAY WITH THE SNOWMAN BUILDING."

"*NEVER* STICK YOUR ARM OUT THE WINDOW OF THE CAR WHEN IT'S MOVING, DEAR."

"ALL RIGHT, WHAT IS IT _THIS_ TIME?!"

"DO ME A FAVOR AND ACT LIKE THERE'S NOTHING WRONG WITH IT. MY DAD'S PRETTY PROUD OF THE FACT THAT HE PUT IT TOGETHER ALL BY HIMSELF."

"WOW! FIRST A DRUM AND NOW CYMBALS! THANKS GRANDMA AND GRANDPA!"

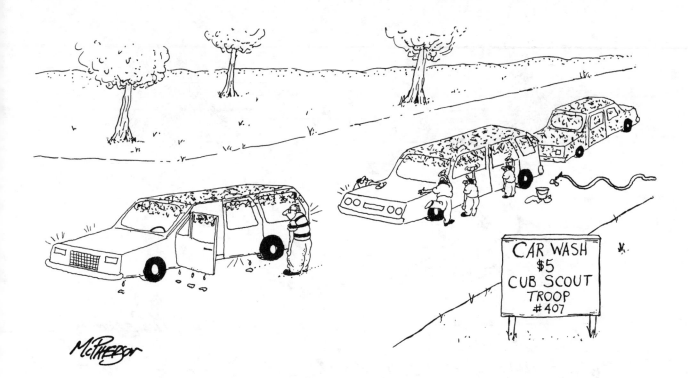

CAR WASH
$5
CUB SCOUT
TROOP
407

"WOW! THAT WAS NEAT, DAD! OK, TEACH ME HOW TO THROW IT! DAD?!"

"FOR CRYIN' OUT LOUD MOM! IT'S ONLY A _SLIDE_!"

"WOW! THAT WAS NEAT! OKAY, TRY IT ON HIGH."

"YOU GOT ANY BRIGHT IDEAS HOW TO GET A PEANUT BUTTER AND JELLY SANDWICH OUT OF THE VCR?"

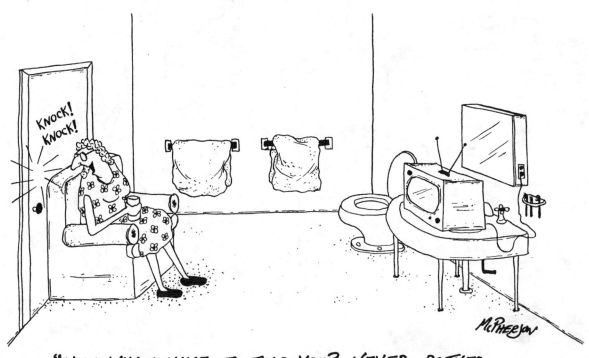

"NOW WHAT HAVE I TOLD YOU? NEVER BOTHER MOMMY WHEN SHE'S IN THE BATHROOM!"

"THIS? THIS IS NINJA TURTLE SOUP."

"NAH, IT'S STILL NOT QUITE RIGHT. PUT IN MORE WORMS."

"YEAH, I KNOW SHE SHOULDN'T PLAY WITH HER FOOD. BUT THAT'S PRETTY GOOD!"

"I'LL TAKE SIX HAMBURGERS, FOUR SMALL FRIES, FOUR COKES, THREE CHOCOLATE SHAKES, AND A HUNDRED NAPKINS."

"AND I BETTER NOT FIND YOU SHAKING THOSE PRESENTS TO TRY AND FIGURE OUT WHAT THEY ARE."

"SORRY MOM. I THOUGHT I HAD ENOUGH MOMENTUM TO CLEAR THE HOUSE."

"I'D LIKE TO REPORT A LOST DAD, ABOUT 45, 5 FEET 9 INCHES TALL, MOSTLY BALD, LAST SEEN IN THE SPORTING GOODS DEPARTMENT, SORT OF NERDY LOOKING, ANSWERS TO THE NAME 'ED'."

"HERE'S PART OF AN OLD CHEESEBURGER AND I THINK
I CAN FEEL A COUPLE MORE FRENCH FRIES!"

"DON'T WORRY ABOUT IT. THE WAY MY DAD DRIVES, HE PROBABLY WON'T EVEN NOTICE IT'S MISSING."

"WOW! I HAVEN'T HEARD DAD SCREAM THAT LOUD SINCE WE CARVED OUR NAMES INTO THE HOOD OF HIS CORVETTE!"

"MY MOM'S TRYING TO GET ME TO STOP
WIPING MY NOSE ON MY SLEEVE."

"I CAN'T BELIEVE YOU ACTUALLY CLEANED UP YOUR ENTIRE ROOM IN FIVE MINUTES!"

"OK! WHO'S THE WISE GUY WHO PUT THE MR. YUK STICKER ON MY TURNIP CASSEROLE?!"

"I HAVE TOLD YOU REPEATEDLY NOT TO SLIDE DOWN THE BANISTER!"

"I HOPE YOU'RE NOT GOING TO HUMILIATE US AGAIN THIS YEAR, MOM, BY PASSING OUT ASPARAGUS AS TREATS."

"WE WERE CONCERNED THAT GETTING A DOG WOULD DISTRACT RONNIE FROM HIS SCHOOL WORK, BUT HIS GRADES IN GEOGRAPHY HAVE ACTUALLY IMPROVED."

"ALL RIGHT DAD! NOW TRY FOUR MEATBALLS!"

"WE'RE TRYING TO DISCOURAGE THE KIDS FROM SITTING TOO CLOSE TO THE TV."

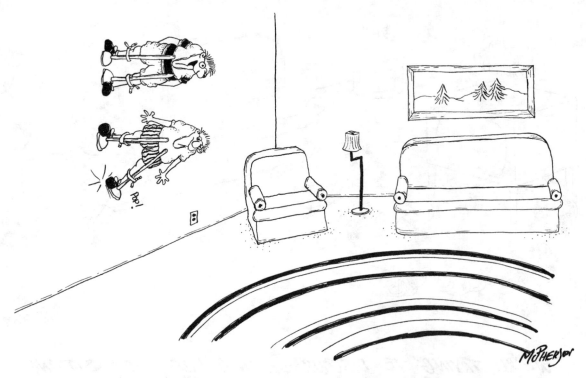

"RACE YA' TO THE DINING ROOM CEILING!"

"I DO <u>NOT</u> WANT YOU FEEDING THE DOG SCRAPS AT THE TABLE!"

"MAYBE OUR PRICE IS TOO HIGH."

"I WAS JUST STANDING THERE IN THE YARD WHEN ART NABCO THREW A SNOWBALL AT ME. SO I THREW ONE BACK. THEN HE THREW A BIGGER ONE BACK AT ME. SO I THREW AN EVEN _BIGGER_ ONE BACK AT HIM...."

"LEAVING HANDPRINTS IS FOR WIMPS."

"FOR HEAVEN'S SAKE! LOOK WHAT YOU'VE DONE! THE NEXT TIME YOU BOYS WANT TO PLAY ARMY YOU GO TO THE PARK!"

"MOM! HELP! DOWN HERE!"

"THIS'LL BE A GOOD CHANCE FOR YOU TO TEST OUT THAT RUST-PROOFING JOB ON THE CAR, HUH DAD?"

"YEAH, IT'S SNOWING PRETTY HARD MRS. NEAL.
I'LL BE HAPPY TO SHOVEL THE DRIVEWAY FOR YOU."

"SORRY ABOUT THIS, MARK. MY FATHER HAS A TENDENCY TO BE A LITTLE OVERPROTECTIVE."

STELLA'S CHANCES OF GETTING A SECOND DATE WITH RANDY BOGMAN TOOK A TURN FOR THE WORSE WHEN HER FATHER STARTED PLAYING THE "GILLIGAN'S ISLAND" THEME SONG ON HIS TEETH.

CHRISTMAS LIGHTS
UNTANGLED
$5

McPHERSON

"FIRST OF ALL DAD, A LAWN MOWER SPEWS ALL KINDS OF TOXINS INTO THE AIR AND DEPLETES THE OZONE LAYER. SECONDLY, GRASS GIVES OFF OXYGEN AND BY CUTTING IT WE LITERALLY CHOKE EVERY LIVING CREATURE. BUT, IF THAT'S WHAT YOU WANT ME TO DO, DAD, I'LL DO IT."

"CHECK IT OUT. I'VE BEEN CUTTING A HALF INCH OFF DAD'S CHAIR LEGS EVERY DAY FOR THE LAST TWO WEEKS."

"I FIGURED SINCE ROB WAS JUST SITTING HERE WAITING FOR YOU TO COME DOWN FOR YOUR DATE, I MIGHT AS WELL PUT HIM TO USE."

"THE FUNNY THING IS, DAD, I WAS ONLY GOING ABOUT 10 MILES PER HOUR."

"ARE YOU TRYING TO DESTROY MY SOCIAL LIFE?! I KNOW PEOPLE AROUND HERE, DAD! PLEASE TAKE OFF THAT STUPID HAT!"

"HEY, WALT. I THINK YOU FORGOT YOUR LUNCH AGAIN."

"SORRY ABOUT THIS. MY DAD WOULDN'T LET ME BORROW THE CAR."

"THIS IS SOME KIND OF A CRUEL JOKE, ISN'T IT DAD?"

"MY DAD SAID IT WAS STUPID TO GO OUT AND PAY 150 BUCKS FOR ROLLERBLADES WHEN HE COULD JUST MAKE ME A PAIR IN THE BASEMENT."

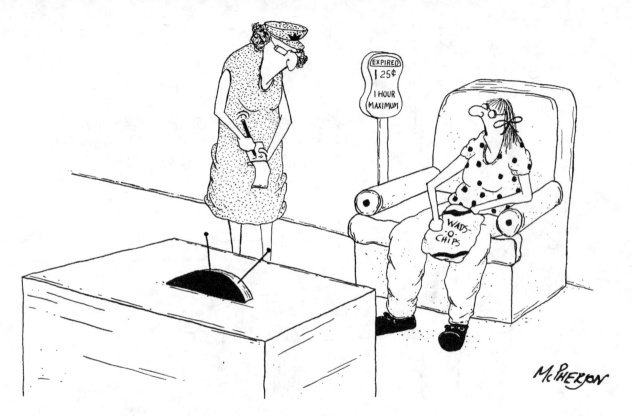

"YOU'RE SERIOUS ABOUT THIS ONE-HOUR-OF-TV-A-NIGHT RULE, AREN'T YOU MOM?!"

"NOW, HERE'S THE FUNNY PART, DAD."

THE OLDER GENERATION FIGHTS BACK.

"LET ME GUESS. YOU WANT ME TO TURN DOWN THE STEREO."